OLD TESTAMENT STORIES

The Kids' Translation

Mark Lawrence

Illustrations
Daniel Jankowski

CSS Publishing Company, Inc., Lima, Ohio

OLD TESTAMENT
STORIES

Copyright © 1997 by
CSS Publishing Company, Inc.
Lima, Ohio

ISBN 0-7880-0768-8

To Elena, Joshua,
Avery, Gail and
Big Daddy Lawrence

Table of Contents

Day One

In a far away time before anything rhymed, God said,
"I'm all alone in this place!"

He gave a command, and lifted His hand. And waved it
through deep outer space.

Then lightning and thunder cracked in a wonder...
Sparks started shooting around!

The Heavens were shaking 'cause God was now making
a place where He'd always be found!

The Earth on its birthday had no bright light-rays.
Outside it was dark and not sunny.

The weather not pleasing, the waters were
freezing...The mountains were lumpy and funny.

But God was not through...
His work was undone.
KA-BOOM!
In a big bang, God created the Sun!

He liked all the bright He made with His might.
He named the light Daytime.
He called the dark Night.

Nothing was worth missing this birth!
On the first day God created the
Heavens and Earth.

There was evening...then morning on Day Number One,
Earth and Heavens glowed, by the light of the Sun.

Day Two
God, the Earth's father, gave a new order
To divide the world's oceans with a new border.

He parted the waters, with a pass of His hand...
The wet He called Seas, the dry He called Land.

His hand passed above, and made Oceans up high.
A cushion for cloud tops, this He called Sky.

The Earth now looked just the way that it should.
God looked down and smiled and knew it was good.

There was evening...then morning on Day Number Two,
When God made land dry and colored the sky blue.

Day Three
The Earth needed shade. Nothing was green.
Then plants began popping up onto the scene...

Trees and big flowers sprang in the air.
Roses, white daisies, and orchids so rare.

From the trees to the weeds all made new seeds,
So on Earth they'd remain.

Carrots, potatoes, small seeds from tomatoes! All to be planted again.

There was evening...then morning on Day Number Three,
The day God made plants, flowers and trees.

Day Four
There yet were no Seasons, no, not one at all.
No Winter, no Springtime, no Summer or Fall.

Till God shouted loud, so the Earth would spin near...
Around the bright Sun, in the time of a year.

Now summers are hot; in winter, snow found.
In springtime, new flowers. Fall...leaves on the ground.

Making seasons was easy. God finished soon.
He looked in the sky, and wished there the Moon!

God looked down on Earth, and loved it all dearly.
But He wasn't finished. No...not even nearly!

The Moon shone brightly as never before...
High in the Heavens on Day Number Four.

Day Five
The land was empty, fish and birds just a starter!
The Earth needed life; God worked much harder.

God made big creatures, and small ones...like ants!
He made lions and tigers, and huge ele*phants.*

God made that day all animals that live.
He was one creature short...our first relative!

There was evening...then morning on Day Number Five,
The day God made the Earth   much more than alive.

Day Six
The sixth day was special 'cause God made us — Man!
We're made from some dust, formed by God's hand.

God blessed all the creatures, and also the man.
He said then, "Go out; multiply in the land."

God then looked around...saw all was okay.
First evening, then morning, to end the Sixth Day.

Day Seven
The work was now done, Earth finished and Heaven.
Which brings us to countdown the last day...Day Seven!

On this day God and His angels did rest.
In all of the Heavens, the Earth's beauty was best.

God asks on Day Seven, we remember the birth
Of man, and all creatures, the Heavens and Earth.

Those first six days working...God made all that you see.
He then gave it away, all to you and to me.

Now if friends ask you why there are stars in the sky,
Tell them you know the whole story...

Of the Heavens and Earth, and their six-day long birth,
Give thanks to God and His glory!

Don't forget the best part of why God would start
This world and all that we see.

While alone out in space, God made Earth as the place...
He'd be closest to you and to me.

During the time God made the earth's land,
He planted a garden — a home for the man.

God named the man Adam. No last name was needed.
God made him from dust from the garden he seeded.

Back at the garden...the home for the man,
God named the home Eden, 'cause that was His plan.

The garden was fun. It was great.   It was neat.
The weather was sunny.
There was plenty to eat.

"All mine?" Adam said. "Oh, thank you, indeed!"
Adam lived in the garden. God met all his needs.

But God gave Adam just one little law...
"You can eat anything, everything,
all that you saw,

But *don't* eat the apples.
Not one from *this* tree,"
And He pointed up high so
Adam could see...

"These apples will hurt you...
Don't take just one bite.
Please do what I tell you,"
He told him that night.

Then God brought Adam
All creatures to name.
Birds, fish, and land dwellers.
No two were the same.

Adam gave names to all of the beasts.
He liked naming birdies. Naming bugs he liked least.

Adam needed a helper but none could be found.
So God made him sleep, a sleep sleepier-than-sound.

While Adam was sleeping, God made him a wife.
Eve was her name. God joined them for life.

Their home was the garden. Adam kept up the lawn.
No school and no work. No clothes to put on.

Adam and Eve, the first man and his wife,
Lived in God's Eden a wonderful life.

So, the greatest grandparents related to you
Were Adam and Eve...from them we all grew.

God was their father. They saw Him each day.
He lived with them in the garden He made.

God is your father...up in Heaven above.
Although you can't see Him, you can feel His love.

Just close your eyes tight at night when you pray.
Ask Him to lead you, and always to stay.

The warmth that you feel is a hug that God gives...
Now your heart is the garden, the place where He lives.

There lived in God's garden, maybe near a green lake,
A most crafty mean creature; they named him a Snake.

The snake always slithered down low— saber-toothed
Telling stories and rumors, but never the truth.

When Eve was out walking
by God's special tree,
The snake said,
"Great apples...
Here, try one. You'll see!"

But Eve knew
the rule God told
Adam that night,
"Those apples
are deadly.
Don't take just
one bite!"

The snake —
he was sneaky —
so what did he say?
He told Eve — God told
him, "One bite is okay."

"Come on...bite the apple.
You'll be just like God!"
Said the snake as he slithered...
and hissed...in the sod.

That day both Adam and Eve were deceived.
They both took a bite from God's apples — retrieved.

Their eyes were now opened...more open than closed.
They saw they were naked...and wearing no clothes!

Both hid in the trees, afraid from the scare.
They sewed fig leaves together — and made underwear!

While God was out walking in the garden He knew,
He was looking for Adam,
He called, "Where are you?"

Adam answered,
"I hear you...but I don't have on clothes.
I'm hiding...I'm naked...from my head to my toes!"

God said,
"You're naked? Just how can that be?"

"I know," God shouted.
"You ate from my tree!"

God said, "Now you've chosen to
live your own life.
You've tasted the apples.
Please leave with your wife."

Adam and Eve packed up all of their goods.
They moved from God's garden —
deep into the woods.

God still loved them...mistakes He forgives.
He made clothes and took them
to the new place they lived.

They broke the one rule, and that made God sad.
But He always would love them...'cause He was their dad.

God also loves you. More than you'll ever know.
He made you in heaven. He's watching you grow.

But, since that day in Eden, mankind works full-time.
Farmers, car-makers...on assembly lines.

So, if somebody asks you why parents do labor,
Tell them the story of the snake with tooth-saber.

That snake, he still whispers...to you and to me.
To trick us...and tell us...to do what we please.

Remember what happened, keep your eyes open wide...
Or you might wind up stranded, lonely, naked...outside!

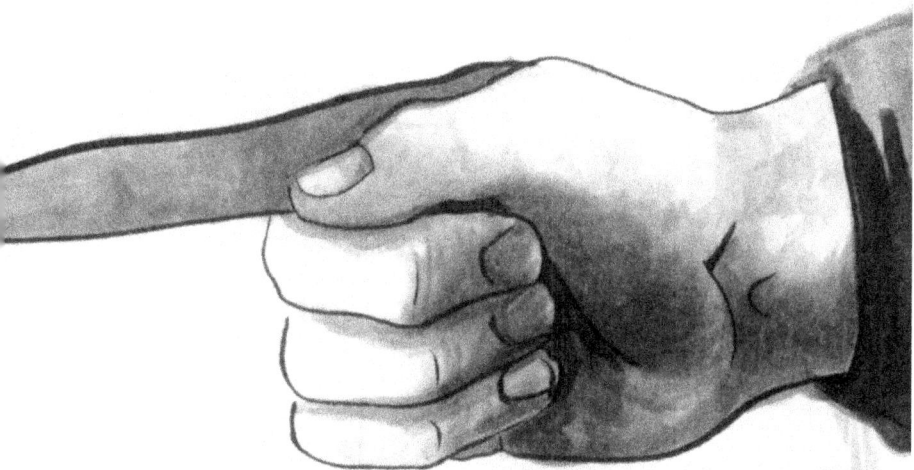

Cain and Abel

Adam and Eve from God's
Eden had run.
They both wanted babies.
Soon Eve had a son.

They named their boy Cain,
but he needed a brother.
So a little while later,
Eve gave birth to another.

The second son, Abel,
God's lambs he did keep.
He worked as a shepherd...
a cowboy for sheep!

While Abel kept sheep,
Cain also worked hard.
He worked as a farmer,
growing fruit in their yard.

The brothers both got
all they ever could need,
From God up in heaven,
who loved them indeed.

As the brothers grew older
they wanted to share
The fruit and sheep
for which they cared.

To share, they both gathered
from all they did keep.
Fruit was Cain's offering...
Abel gave sheep.

Abel gave God the best
sheep he had.
He was happy to give them
'cause it made God glad...

Cain shared with God,
but kept all the best.
He gave God his leftovers,
and kept all the rest!

To God Cain was selfish,
and it made Him sad...
'Cause God gave Cain all the
things he ever had.

Do you have a toy that
you think is best?
Do you hold it and love
it more than the rest?

What if a good friend
comes over to play,
And asks you to share it?
Just what would you say?

Don't forget about Abel,
the boy who believed...
It is better to *give*
than it is to *receive*.

The Lord loves your *gifts*,
in any amount.
The size does not *matter*; the
thought is what counts.

o, if giving God presents,
ike Abel, be smart...
he best gift for
od will come
om your heart!

Many years passed until Noah we saw,
Adam was Noah's Great-Great-Great-Great-Great-
Great-Great-Great-Great-Great-Grandpa!

This was not a good time...men made God sad.
They cheated, told stories. Did all that was bad.

God looked back in time, with His vision so strong.
He wondered out loud, "Where did I go wrong?"

All men were now mean, and that broke God's heart.
He planned to flood earth, and give it a new start.
Before God began to start making rain,
He heard a faint prayer within His domain.

The prayer was from Noah – Adam's his grandpa above.
Thanking God always, Noah asked for God's love.

Noah found favor in the eyes of the Lord.
One man among millions, who sought God's reward.

God told Noah to build a big boat.
A place in the flood where his family would float.

To keep animals alive God knew what to do...
Bring two of each creature. A boat-floating zoo!

A huge boat Noah built. As big as a park!
The neighbors all laughed. They called it an Ark.

After loading the creatures,
God shut the Ark's door.
The skies then got darker,
And it started to pour!
Forty days and forty nights,
God made the skies rain.
The whole earth was now flooded.
No dry land remained!

Those mean people who thought Noah off his rocker
Weren't laughing much now, in Davy Jones' Locker!

Only Noah was left, and those in his boat.
The earth was now empty...'cause bad people don't float.

The bad people gone, the world was now better.
Five months underwater, things couldn't get wetter!

As the waters departed, on a big rock the Ark sat.
A freshly washed mountain, they named Ararat.

Noah opened an Ark window hoping to see,
If birds he let out would go and fly free.

Two times birds left, then flew back to his hand.
The third time a dove flew...
and returned from dry land!

In the dove's mouth, a leaf plucked from a tree.
Noah knew finally: Dry land it did see.

The next day the dove flew, and did not come back.
Noah knew it was time for the Ark to unpack!

God blessed Noah's family and said, "Multiply.
I saved all of your family. My name you did cry."

The Lord then said a remarkable thing...
"Never again a flood covering the earth will I bring."

God did not like what He'd done, it appears...
Some say all those raindrops were really God's tears.
Now after it rains you can look in the air
And see a big promise that God has put there.

A rainbow of colors in the sky can be found
That stretches from Heaven, right down to the ground.

The rainbow you see in the sky as it bends
Shows the love and forgiveness God promised won't end.

So if you should see God's bright bow in the air,
Remember Noah's story and the power of prayer.